Bradwell's Boc

Sussex

a Feast of Fun, Facts and History!

Published by Bradwell Books

11 Orgreave Close Sheffield S13 9NP

Email: books@bradwellbooks.co.uk

Compiled by Camilla Zajac

British Library Cataloguing in Publication Data: a catalogue record for this book is available from the British Library.

1st Edition

ISBN: 9781912060542

Design by: Andrew Caffrey

Print: Gomer Press, Llandysul, Ceredigion SA44 4JL

Photograph Credits: iStock, Creative Commons (CC), and credited individually. Cartoons Tim O'Brien

Cover Photographs Credits: Left - Right. iStock, CC, iStock, iStock, iStock & CC. Main: iStock

BIOGRAPHY

CAMILLA ZAJAC is an author and copywriter who wrangles with words for publishers and companies in sectors as varied as engineering, telematics and manufacturing.

Find out more at:
www.greenlightcopywriting.co.uk

Bradwell's Book of

Sussex

a Feast of Fun, Facts and History!

BRADWELL
BOOKS

Contents

6

INTRODUCTION

Ancient and picturesque, Sussex has been shaped by its fierce sense of independence for many years. Find out how this strong sense of identity has given rise to many fascinating customs and impressive achievements.

17

WIT AND HUMOUR

Have a giggle with some Sussex-based jokes and stories.

32

RECIPES

Sussex is celebrated for its food, so much so that it was said that to venture into the county was to risk being turned into a pudding yourself! Read on for some mouth-watering recipes.

10

DIALECT

The dialect of Sussex has been well preserved. Discover more here and test your talent for 'speaking Sussex'.

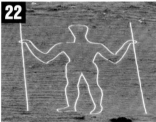

22

HISTORY

From the Battle of Hastings to the birthplace of one of the country's best-loved plays, discover more about the rich history of Sussex.

40

CUSTOMS

Sussex is packed full of fascinating folklore and customs. Whether it is the power of bees, the tradition of gooding or ringing the bull, you can find out more in this book.

GHOST STORIES

From royal spectres to haunted B&Bs and ghostly fights, Sussex is packed with otherworldly goings-on, if the tales are to be believed. Read on – if you dare!

MURDER STORIES

Learn about the tragic events behind two real-life tales of murder from Sussex.

SPORT

The world has Sussex to thank for the invention of cricket. We take a brief look at its history and some lesser-known games and sports that originated in the county.

LEGENDS

Sussex is full of fascinating legends, from myths about Sussex mud to curious stories about the local sheep.

FAMOUS NAMES

Whether it is one of the best-known brands on the high street, the birth of television or the very beginnings of online shopping, Sussex is a place where great things happen!

FAMOUS LOCALS

Sussex people have had and continue to have a considerable influence on the world. Learn about some of the locals who have gone on to great things.

Introduction

'SHE REMINDED HERSELF THAT SUSSEX, WHEN ALL WAS SAID AND DONE, WAS NOT QUITE LIKE OTHER COUNTIES'. STELLA GIBBONS, *Cold Comfort Farm*

God gives all men all earth to love,
But since man's heart is small,
Ordains for each one spot shall
prove Beloved over all.
Each to his choice, and I rejoice
The lot has fallen to me
In a fair ground – In a fair ground –
Yea, Sussex by the Sea!

EXCERPT FROM 'SUSSEX' BY RUDYARD KIPLING

The ancient land of the **South Saxons,** now called **Sussex**, is one of the most beautiful and culturally vibrant areas in southern England. Its spectacular coastline and sunny weather made Sussex one of the first counties to promote and exploit the 18th-century fad for sea-bathing which began the British love for the seaside. The county's rolling countryside and pretty villages have attracted tourists for centuries and it became a rural second home for the BLOOMSBURY GROUP among others. A major portion of Britain's newest National Park, the **South Downs**, is contained within Sussex. Of course, today one should not really talk about Sussex as a single entity (though we will do so for the purposes of this book).

There are two modern counties, **East Sussex** and **West Sussex**, between which is sandwiched the unitary authority of Brighton & Hove.

Sussex has long celebrated having a distinct identity from the rest of the country. Its location has helped to define this character and protected it from the disruption of historic political shifts. In fact, the people of Sussex have such a keen sense of independence that the county's unofficial motto is *We wunt be druv*, which roughly means *'We won't be pushed around.'* It is thought that this motto originates from the picturesque Weald area of the county. You can read more about the motto and its inclusion in Victor Cook's well-loved poem in the history section of this book.

However, Sussex is known for even more than independence and a strong sense of identity. It is also recognised for its well-established bonfire celebrations, which take place across the county to mark both Guy Fawkes Night and the burning of seventeen Protestant martyrs in Lewes between 1555 and 1557. Sussex is a creative place and likes to lead the way, as is motto suggests, in celebrating music and in the fact that it is home to one of the UK's largest and oldest gay pride parades, **Brighton Pride**. Sussex people officially celebrate **Sussex Day** on 16th June. This is the feast day of Sussex's patron saint, St Richard of Chichester, and it has been observed since 2007.

Sussex is full of fascinating customs. Its seaside location and heritage are celebrated in many fishing-related customs. For example, Brighton fishermen say of their Hastings counterparts that when it is time to get up in the morning, they hold a lighted candle outside the window. If the candle blows out they will shake their heads and declare, *"Tain't safe to go out, for there be a gale blowin'.'* On the other hand, if the candle stays alight they will conclude, *"Tain't no good goin' off, for there bain't no wind!'* In either eventuality, they return to their beds.

Sussex is home to many important historic sites, some of which are associated with unnerving ghost stories. Whether it is EASTBOURNE PIER or the ruins of COWDRAY HOUSE, Sussex is the location of many ghostly goings-on, if the stories are to be believed. But Sussex is as much as about the future as it is about the past. After all, this is the place where TV first flickered into life and where online shopping was first conceived and created. It is the birthplace of cricket and it's the home of an internationally renowned marbles competition. It is the place that gave rise to one of our best-loved singers, as well as an important cookery writer and a leading feminist.

There is far too much to share about Sussex than will fit in this little book. But we hope that it gives you a flavour of all that is Sussex.

HAPPY EXPLORING!

Bognor seafront from the pier, 1890
West Sussex Past picture archive

Sussex DIALECT

Although dialects are still evident in everyday speech from different parts of the country, they are nowhere near as common or as diverse as they used to be.

This gradual extinction has been noted and mourned by writers and antiquarians over many years, and huge efforts have been made to capture the colloquial speech of men and women from various parts of the country.

The county of Sussex has been a particular focus for these efforts. Dialect was preserved in some areas well into the twentieth century, helped by the county's relative geographical inaccessibility behind the physical barriers of the **Sussex Downs** and the ancient forest of the **Weald**. This section represents some words, phrases and anecdotes gathered from many different sources.

PRONUNCIATION AND USAGE

As in many rural areas, the pronunciation of Sussex dialect words and names was markedly different from their urban or received versions, sometimes resulting in confusion for outsiders. The true Sussex man divides the world into two parts – Sussex (and maybe Kent, at a push) and the rest or the world, which is known as the *Sheeres*. The term is not restricted geographically – as well as applying to neighbouring counties and other parts of the UK, China and Australia have both been described as being in the Sheeres. Foreigners (from anywhere other than Sussex or Kent) are known as *Sheere-men*, and may not be guaranteed a friendly welcome. Sussex place names ending in *'ly'* are often pronounced *'lie'*, rather than the

Fetching wood in the snow, near Hastings, c.1890
George Woods, East Sussex Library Archive

more usual *'lee'*. A pair of old rhyming couplets illustrate this:

Hellingly, Chiddingly and Hoathly,
Three lies, and all of them true.

If in Sussex you be,
Then it's Chiddinglie, not Chiddinglee.

Indeed, the *'eye'* pronunciation is also heard in the common use of the word *'sureleye'*, used in many situations to add particular emphasis to a sentence. This and other oddities are described in the following advice to those from foreign parts:

If true Sussex you would be,
Say sureleye, not surely.
In names of places stress should dwell
Upon the final syllable.
Thus, Ardingleye doth well accord
With Southwick, Berwick and Seaford.

During the nineteenth century there was a fashion for writing poetry in local dialect. RICHARD LOWER, a schoolmaster at Chiddingly, wrote a number of dialect poems; this is an extract from *Tom Cladpole's Journey to Lunnon*, published in 1830:

Many long miles I shuffled on,
As fast as I could goo;
At last I gun to feel, ya see,
De haboot ring ma toe.

A liddle aluss stood close by –
Thinks I, I'll go in here
And git, ya see, a coger loike,
Ov good brencheese an' beer.

In Sussex dialect, gender is almost always feminine. There's an old saying: *'Everything in Sussex is a she except a tom cat, and she's a he.'*

Middling is a useful word in Sussex, possessing many different meanings. It may mean *'very much'*, as in *'He lashed out middling, I can tell ye!'* It may mean *'quite well'*, as in *'She turned out purty middling.'* It may even mean *'terribly bad'*, as in *'How was the wedding?' 'Middling, thank ye.' 'What, only middling?' 'Yes – you see, the parson he entirely forgot about it, and he'd gone away, so we was forced to wait in church two hours.'*

Quick is another multi-purpose word, with many meanings. It can mean pregnant, or else it may mean alive: *'I thought the sheep was dead when I first saw it, but I found it was quick still.'* It can also mean to hurry: *'I'll quick him fast enough if he doesn't quick himself a little more.'*

When it is applied to the sands of the Sussex beaches, it can also mean unsafe and insecure for walking or riding: *'You should not ride on the sands so soon after the tide has turned, for they are sure to be quick and shifting.'*

iStock

Glossary

A

Abed – in bed

About as common – in reasonable health

Abroad – in all directions, all around

Absit – absent

Ache – to tire of something

Ackle – fit

Adder's spear – a large dragonfly

B

Babbins – wood used for fire-lighting

Bachelor's button – the pink clematis

Backstays, backsters or flappers – wide flat pieces of wood, similar to snow shoes, used by fishermen to cross shingle beaches or soft mud

Bawl – to read aloud
Said a mother of her child, kept off school because of illness: *'I keeps him to his book all the same, and his father likes to hear him bawl a bit in the evening.'*

Beat the Devil round the gooseberry bush – tell a long story or rigmarole without much point to it
An old man in Rye was heard to complain that he didn't think the new curate was much of a hand in the pulpit, he did beat the Devil round the gooseberry bush so.

C

Cackleberry – an egg

Caddling – looking around for odd jobs

Cadey – a hat

Cadger – anyone given to begging

Caffincher – chaffinch

Caterwise – diagonally

Catterning – the custom of begging for apples and beer on St. Catherine's Day

Chop-backs – a derogatory name given to Hastings fishermen by the fishermen of other towns

D

Dallop – a parcel of tea, packed for smuggling

Derricking – the technique of hauling goods up cliffs from inaccessible beaches

Devil's children – magpies

Disremember – to forget

Dobbs or Master Dobbs – a house-fairy who does all sorts of domestic work

'Master Dobbs has been helping you!' – a common expression used when someone has done more work than expected.

Dumbledore – the bumble bee Dumbledores are said to have a spear in their tail, but in Sussex a bee is always said to bite, rather than sting.

E

Egger-nogger – sleet (a seafaring term)

F

Fall – autumn

Certain old Sussex dialect words crossed the Atlantic with the early settlers to end up in common usage in the United States.

Flindermouse, flittermouse or fluttermouse – bat

Fluttergrub – a man who enjoys working with the earth and getting into a mess

G

Gifts – white specks which appear on the fingernails, supposedly indicating the arrival of a present

A gift on the thumb is sure to come, A gift on the finger is sure to linger.

H

Hagtracks – circles of coarse green grass, seen in meadows and on the Downs, said to be the tracks of dancing witches or fairies

Hobbledick – a spirit said to live in elder trees, who must be consulted before they are cut down

I

Item – a hint or a clue

J

January butter – one of many terms for Sussex mud, renowned for being sticky and heavy, particularly over the Weald

Jawled out – tired, fatigued

Jug – a Brighton fisherman

Juggy – a squirrel

K

Kettle broth – bread with salt and pepper in hot water

Kime or kine – a weasel

Knap, knep or kneb – a small hill

Knucker – a water dragon. One such lived in Knucker Hole at Lyminster, near Arundel

Knucker Hole – a pond reputed to be bottomless

L

Laurence or Old Laurence – a mysterious personage who is supposed to influence people and cause idleness or laziness

'Old Laurence has got a hold o' me.'

Lawyer – a long shoot of bramble, thick and vigorous and covered in thorns

'When once a lawyer gets a holt an ye, ye don't easy get shut of 'em.'

M

Mullet – a person born and bred in Arundel, so called because of the many mullet fish to be found in the River Arun

N

Notch – a run in cricket

The old countryside custom was to keep tally by cutting notches in a stick.

O

Owlet – a moth

P

Particular – unwell

'He's lookin' very particular; I don't like the look on 'em.'

Pathery – silly; applied especially to sheep

Print moonlight – very clear moonlight, almost as clear as daylight

'Well, he must have been primed to fall into the pond such a night as that was, for t'was print moonlight.'

Q

Quick – a useful word with many meanings: pregnant, alive, to hurry, or (when applied to sands) insecure and unsafe to walk on

R

Recollects – memory
'I quite lost my recollects.'

S

Scraze – when falling over, to scratch and bruise at the same time
'She was climmin' up after some scads and she fell down and scrazed her knees.'
Snuffy – angry

T

Tissick – a ticklish but persistent cough

Punch cures the gout, the colic and the tissick,
And it is agreed to be the very best of physic.

U

Unaccountable – a favourite all-purpose word, often used as an adjective by Sussex folk. Often used to mean exceedingly or excessively

V

Vent – a place where several roads meet (pronounced 'went')

W

Warp – four herrings, two in each hand, a measure used in the days when fish were counted by hand. Thirty-three warps were reckoned to equal a hundred.

Wild – people who live in the Downs always refer to the Weald of Sussex as the Wild, and its inhabitants as the Wild People

Y

Yaffle – the green woodpecker

Humour

Chris and Colin were long-time neighbours in Nutley. Every time Chris saw Colin coming round to his house, his heart sank. This was because he knew that, as always, Colin would be visiting him in order to borrow something, and he was fed up with it.

'I'm not going to let Colin get away with it this time,' he said quietly to his wife.

'Watch what I'm about to do.'

'Hi there. I wondered if you were thinking about using your hedge trimmer this afternoon?' asked Colin.

'Oh, I'm very sorry,' said Chris, trying to look apologetic, *'but I'm actually going to be using it all this afternoon.'*

'In that case,' responded Colin with a big grin, *'you won't be using your golf clubs… mind if I borrow them?'*

'My wife and I went on a sail-making holiday in Sussex last summer.'
'Firle?'
'At the end of the process, yes, but mainly sewing.'

....

'I got a wine gum stuck to my shoe when I was rambling through a lovely village in East Sussex.'
'Maynards Green?'
'Couldn't tell – it was squashed and covered in mud.'

....

'My wife went to a small village in mid-Sussex'
'Newick?'
'No. Never heard of it before!'

....

It was the day before the Battle of Hastings. King Harold asked his top man in the army, *'Are my troops ready?'*
'Yes, Your Majesty', said the man. *'Shall we give you a demonstration?'*
'Yes, please', replied the King. The man got all the archers lined up and instructed them to fire. Thousands of arrows flew through the air and landed accurately. However, one archer fired straight up into the air. The arrow flew up hundreds of feet, turned round and came back down again, landing just a few inches from where King Harold was standing.
'You want to watch him', said the King. *'If he's not careful, he'll have somebody's eye out tomorrow!'*

....

A man walked into a chip shop and said, *'Hello. I'd like a steak and kiddely pie, please.'*
The woman behind the counter said, *'What was that?'*
'I'd like a steak and kiddely pie.'
'I'm very sorry sir, what did you say?'
'I WANT A STEAK AND KIDDELY PIE!!'
'Do you mean "steak and kidney" pie?'
'I said kiddely, diddle I?!'

(The steak and kidney pudding was first created in Sussex)

What beverage do Lewes F.C. players drink?
Penal-tea!

....

Two rival cricketers from Stonewall Park and Flimwell were having a chat. *'The local team wants me to play for them very badly,'* said the man from Kent.
'Well,' said his friend, *'you're just the man for the job then.'*

....

The nervous young batsman playing for Mayfield was having a very bad day. In a quieter moment in the game, he muttered to one of his teammates, *'Well, I suppose you've seen worse players.'*
There was no response...so he said it again. *'I said I guess you've seen worse players.'*
His teammate looked at him and answered: *'I heard you the first time. I was just trying to think…'*

A priest was walking along the Seven Sisters cliffs when he came upon two locals pulling a man from Kent ashore on the end of a rope.
'That's what I like to see,' said the priest. *'A man helping his fellow man.'*
As he was walking away, one local remarked to the other, *'Well, he certainly doesn't know the first thing about shark fishing.'*

....

One day, a father and his son arrived at the ground to watch Dover RFC play Hove Rugby Club. But the man suddenly realised that he couldn't find their tickets for the game, so he said to his son, *'Nip home and see if I left the tickets there.'*
His son replied, *'No probs, Dad'* and set off.
Half an hour later Bobby returned to his dad, who was patiently waiting outside the ground, and said, *'Yep, they're on the kitchen table where you left them.'*

A man from Arundel once bought two horses, but soon realised that he couldn't tell them apart. So he asked the farmer who lived next door what he should do. The farmer suggested he measure them.

The man came back triumphantly and said: *'The white horse is two inches taller than the black horse!'*

There are many good things to come out of Kent – most of them roads leading to Sussex.

Two blokes from Hastings went into a pub.

The first man said, *'A pint o' bitter, and a half o' shandy for my mate Donkey, please!'*

The publican replied. *'What's with him calling you Donkey?'*

The second one said, *'Oh, 'e aw, 'e aw, 'e always calls me that!'*

A rather cocky man working on a busy construction site in East Grinstead was bragging that he could outdo anyone in a feat of strength. He made a special case of making fun of Morris, one of the more senior workmen. After several minutes, Morris had had enough.

'Why don't you put your money where your mouth is?' he said. *'I'll bet a week's wages that I can haul something in a wheelbarrow over to that outbuilding that you won't be able to wheel back.'*

'You're on, mate!' the overconfident young man replied. *'It's a bet! Let's see what you got.'*

Morris reached out and grabbed the wheelbarrow by the handles. Then, nodding to the young man, he said, *'All right. Get in.'*

A life-long career man tired of his daily commute from Worthing to London decided he was going to give up his old life, move to the country, and become a chicken farmer. He bought a chicken farm in Bodiam and moved in. It turned out that his next-door neighbour was also a chicken farmer. The neighbour came for a visit one day and said, *'Chicken farming isn't easy. I know. To help you get started, I'll give you 100 chickens.'*

The new chicken farmer was delighted. Two weeks later the neighbour dropped by to see how things were going. The new farmer said, *'Not too well mate. All 100 chickens died.'*

The neighbour said, *'Oh, I can't believe that. I've never had any trouble with my chickens. I'll give you 100 more.'*

Another two weeks went by and the neighbour dropped in again. The new farmer said, *'You're not going to believe this, but the second 100 chickens died too.'*

Astounded, the neighbour asked, *'What went wrong?'*

The new farmer said, *'Well, I'm not sure whether I'm planting them too deep or too close together.'*

Sussex HISTORY

Sussex is rich in history. Here was fought the most decisive conflict in British history: the Battle of Hastings, which ushered in the Norman age.

Despite the name, the **Battle of Hastings** did not actually take place in Hastings. It was fought six miles away at a place called SENLAC HILL. While this gave Harold a strategic advantage, the Saxons were eventually beaten. BATTLE ABBEY, founded to commemorate WILLIAM THE CONQUEROR'S triumph, is just one of the very many important and impressive historical sites to be found in Sussex. The county is especially blessed with castles, some of the best preserved and most beautiful to be found anywhere in Britain. Then there are the elegant houses of the Regency period which remind us of the coastal towns' popularity with the aristocracy of two centuries ago.

You may sometimes hear references to 'Silly Sussex'. However, among themselves Sussex folk are proud of their intelligence and resourcefulness, and indeed the description is thought to derive from saelig, an Anglo-Saxon word meaning holy, blessed or good. SAELIG SUSSEX therefore means 'The Holy Land of the South'.

Silly or not, Sussex folk are well known for being stubborn. It is said that Sussex itself is pig-shaped, with the snout at RYE in the east, the legs at BEACHY HEAD and SELSEY BILL and the rear at UPPARK in the west, and Sussex folk can match their county in terms of their pig-headedness. As we have already seen, it is well known that a

Battle Abbey - iStock

Sussex man *'wunt be druv'*; indeed, W. VICTOR COOK celebrated this maxim in his 1914 poem:

Some folks as come to Sussex,
They reckons as they know
A durn sight better what to do
Than simple folks, like me and you
Could possibly suppose.
But them as comes to Sussex,
They mustn't push and shove,
For Sussex will be Sussex,
And Sussex won't be druv!

Until relatively recently William the Conqueror, the victor at the Battle of Hastings in 1066 and the first of the great Norman Kings of England, was still known by Sussex folk as DUKE WILLIAM, or the DUKE OF NORMANDY. This persistence may be explained by the relative geographical isolation of Sussex, separated from the rest of the mainland by the great upland sweep of the Weald, so that the folk memory of Duke William's landing and the great battle at Hastings was preserved intact for much longer than elsewhere in England.

Another historical oddity is connected with the 29th of May, which used to be known throughout England as **Oak Apple Day** *(or Royal Oak Day)*, commemorating the date of CHARLES II's triumphant return to London and the Restoration of the English Monarchy in 1660. In Sussex, however, it was known rather more irreverently as **Pinch Bum Day**, in memory of COLONEL WILLIAM CARELESS, who hid with King Charles in the Royal Oak at BOSCOBEL in Shropshire, and had to keep pinching His Royal Highness on his noble posterior to keep him awake and stop him falling out of the tree. Sussex folk would also chastise those who did not *'sport their oak'* (wear a sprig of oak or an oak apple) by slashing the backs of their legs with stinging nettles.

A Moving Cathedral

ARUNDEL in West Sussex is famed for its stunning cathedral, the CATHEDRAL CHURCH OF OUR LADY AND ST. PHILIP HOWARD. This impressive building is worth a visit for many reasons, not least for its somewhat surprising connection with the precursor to the modern taxi. This is because it was designed by JOSEPH HANSOM, the inventor of the Hansom cab. The Hansom cab was a horse-drawn carriage that replaced the hackney carriage as a safe and affordable way for people to travel. The word *'cab'* is a shortened version of the word *'cabriolet'*, which relates to the way the carriage was designed. It was only later, with the introduction of clockwork mechanical taximeters to measure fares, that the name became *'taxicab'*.

The importance of being in Worthing Sussex has a close association with one of the country's best-loved plays. This is because OSCAR WILDE wrote *The Importance of Being Earnest* while spending the summer of 1895 in Worthing with his family. No wonder the main character in the play is called JACK WORTHING!

A Popular Anthem

'And did those feet in ancient time' is the opening line of what is probably WILLIAM BLAKE'S most famous poem, thanks to it being sung at public events like school prize days and football matches. Known popularly as *'Jerusalem'*, and set to rousing music by SIR HUBERT PARRY in 1916, the song is considered by some to be the country's true national anthem. Blake wrote the poem while he was living in FELPHAM, near BOGNOR REGIS, between 1800 and 1803. Although he was initially relatively happy in the area, he eventually fell out with a soldier who trespassed in his garden. This led to a trial for treason in CHICHESTER, though thankfully Blake was successfully defended.

THE LONG MAN OF WILMINGTON

Sussex is rich in ancient history. Possibly its most famous ancient site is the **Long Man of Wilmington**, which is 235 feet (more than 20 metres) tall. As you would expect for what is the largest representation of the human form in Europe, this human hill figure is a stunning sight. Situated on WINDOVER HILL near WILMINGTON in East Sussex, it used to be known as the *'Wilmington Giant'*, or as the *'Green Man'* by locals. Yet this Scheduled Ancient Monument is still a mystery thanks a lack of clear historical evidence. While many originally believed that it was of prehistoric origins, others thought that it was created by a monk some time between the 11th and 15th centuries. Investigations undertaken in 2003 suggest that the figure was created in the 16th or 17th century AD.

The Long Man of Wilmington - iStock

While it looks from a distance to have been carved from the chalk hillside, the figure today is formed from painted breeze blocks and lime mortar. The Long Man is not the only hill figure in EAST SUSSEX, however, as the county also has the **Litlington White Horse**.

ROMAN DELIGHTS

Another important heritage site in Sussex is FISHBOURNE ROMAN PALACE AND GARDENS in CHICHESTER. This is the biggest single Roman site unearthed in Britain and covers no less than six acres. To put that into perspective, it covers more ground than BUCKINGHAM PALACE! Built in the first century AD, the palace was lived in up until its destruction in a huge fire in around AD 270. Today, the site reveals a fascinating story about Roman life, from the largest collection of early Roman mosaic floors in Britain, including the much-loved *'Cupid on a Dolphin'*, to its ancient underfloor heating system. Incredibly, the palace was only discovered in 1960 by an engineer laying a new water main across a field!

A HISTORIC EMBLEM

Sussex has a heraldic shield with which it has been associated since the 17th century. This shield features a mythical bird – THE MARTLET. Six martlets are depicted on a blue background. The martlet image is of course a stylised depiction of a bird and symbolises the constant quest for knowledge. It is thought that the word comes originally from the bird known as the martin, with the diminutive *'-let'* ending making it mean *'little martin'*. The design of the heraldic shield went on to become the basis of the flag of Sussex and the armorial bearings granted to the county councils of East and West Sussex. However, it is not an official Coat of Arms. The first surviving record of it in use was in 1611 when cartographer JOHN SPEED used it to represent the Kingdom of the South Saxons in his atlas, *The Theatre of the Empire of Great Britaine.*

FISHING, SMUGGLING AND THE SEA

Sussex has a rich maritime heritage. From BOSHAM and THE WITTERINGS in the west to CAMBER in the east, the coast and the sea have provided a living for generations of families who have fished and worked the shores, as well as sometimes engaging in other more nefarious practices involving dark nights and barrels of contraband goods.

Fishermen from different towns and villages often have names for each other. The men of HASTINGS are known as *chop-backs* by fishermen from other places, but the Hastings folk are not proud of this nickname.

Times were when everyone in Sussex who lived within reach of the coast was in some way connected with smuggling, or *'the Trade'*, as it was known. These activities were never regarded as dishonest, being instead viewed as work carried out in answer to the introduction of unpopular taxes which were seen as an infringement of liberty. Labourers were always ready to help whenever darkness fell, farmers allowed their horses to be borrowed for the night, and vicars would make no mention of mysterious barrels which took up temporary residence in church vaults. Even the excisemen sometimes collaborated for a price, but when disagreements arose and men came to blows the doctor tended to wounds for nothing, and never enquired about the provenance of the cases of tea or kegs of brandy which appeared on his doorstep at daybreak. Rudyard Kipling, who lived in the heart of smuggling country, knew very well that the policy was to *'watch the wall, my darling, while the gentlemen go by'.*

Some villages were particularly well known for their collaboration with the smugglers. In YAPTON villagers would leave their doors open so that smugglers could make a fast getaway if the excisemen were on their tail. This is still remembered today when careless folk may well be berated for leaving doors standing open with the cry: *'Close that door! Do you come from Yapton?'*

One story goes that in the 18th century there was a well-known smuggling gang, known as the RUXLEY CREW, who operated out of Hastings. They were successful at their illicit trade but became greedy and decided to try a spot of piracy to boost their earnings. They took to boarding likely-looking vessels that had been becalmed, overcoming the crew and taking all the valuables and money they could carry.

One day they tried their trick on a large Dutch merchantman, but they were driven back by a spirited defence from the crew and one of their number was taken prisoner. Back ashore

A fisherman in traditional clothing on Hastings beach, c.1890
George Woods, East Sussex Library Archive

they gathered extra support from among the Hastings fishermen and returned in greater numbers, this time succeeding in overpowering the crew. However, not content with robbing the ship, the Hastings men led by the Ruxley Crew took revenge on the Dutch captain in a particularly vicious manner. They killed him by chopping up and down his back with an axe – hence the unpopular nickname for the men of the town.

RACING AT GATWICK

As hard as it might be to imagine now, some of the land on which GATWICK AIRPORT stands was once a racecourse! GATWICK RACECOURSE operated from 1891 to 1940. The GRAND NATIONAL was even run there from 1916 to 1918. Gatwick was first used for aviation in 1928 and opened as Gatwick Airport in June 1958. Next time you set off for your holidays from Gatwick, try to imagine horses racing nearby!

Local *Recipes*

The Seven Good Things of Sussex

Of a score of good things found outside heaven

The land of Sussex was granted seven

The choicest of those I often feel

Is the oily, glutinous Pulborough eel

Though the Selsea cockle would be the best

The Chichester lobster's the lordliest dish

The herring of Rye is the tastiest dish

The mullet of Arundel would have my vote

If I could but forget the Amberley trout

The wheatear of Bourne whenever it's about.

Folk poem

Note: *This is an old poem; the Wheatear is a protected species and we are not advocating catching or eating them!*

Sussex Pond Pudding

Ingredients

For the suet pastry:

225g/8oz of self-raising flour

115g/4oz suet shredded (fresh or packet)

60g/2oz fresh white breadcrumbs

½ tsp sea salt

125ml/scant ¼ pint milk.

For the filling:

1 large lemon

115g/4oz of natural brown sugar

115g/4oz of butter.

Sussex Pond Pudding - iStock

Method

Making the Suet Pastry

Sieve the flour into a mixing bowl and add the salt, then mix in the breadcrumbs. If you're using fresh suet chop it up very small, until it resembles breadcrumbs. Mix the suet into the flour and make a well in the centre. Next, gradually mix in the milk until the dough is soft. Then turn the dough out onto a lightly floured work surface and knead it gently until it is free from cracks. Add more flour if you need to, in order to stiffen the dough so that it looks like light pastry.

Method

Grease a 850ml (1½) pint pudding basin thickly with butter.

Next, roll out the suet crust pastry into a large circle on a floured work surface. Using a sharp knife, cut out a quarter segment of the pastry circle and put it to one side to use as the pudding lid. Place the remaining pastry into the greased pudding basin to create the lining and press the cuts together to seal.

Next, pack half the butter flakes and half the sugar into the bottom of the suet crust lining. Place the whole lemon on top of this, having washed it, trimmed the ends and pricked the surface a sharp skewer. Then cover it with the remaining butter and sugar.

Roll out the set aside quarter of pastry into a circle to fit as a lid to the pudding. Damp it around the edges with a little water and place it on top of the pudding and press the edges to seal them. Pack the pudding down gently.

The level of the pudding should be around 3cm/1inch below the top of the basin - or less. Cut a round, large sheet of greaseproof paper and another slightly larger one of foil so they will extend at least 10cm/4 inches over the sides of the basin.

Next, place the baking parchment on top of the foil and fold a large pleat down the centre of both (to allow for any pudding expansion). Place the sheets over the top of the pudding basin (foil side up) and secure around the sides with string. Wrap the string around the pudding basin several times and tie it off to ensure that the foil top is secured down firmly.

Cut off any excess foil and paper if it is too long. You can also create a basic string handle by looping it over the top and tying it off under the string going around the basin.

Stand the pudding basin in a deep saucepan (with a tight-fitting lid) on an upturned heatproof plate to raise it off the bottom of the saucepan.

Add a little water under the plate to remove any air pockets. Pour in boiling water so that it comes just under half way up the side of the pudding basin.

Keep the water at a medium simmer and a gentle bubble, cover with a tight-fitting lid and steam for three and half hours, topping up with boiling water from time to time. Be sure to check the level of the water regularly to make sure that the pan doesn't run dry.

When the time is up, simply remove the string, foil and greaseproof paper and turn the pudding out carefully on to a shallow dish or plate with a rim. Cut it into slices with a sharp knife and serve it hot with custard, cream, or a traditional lemon sauce.

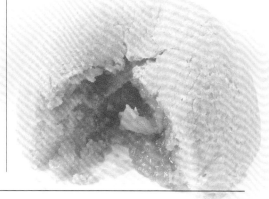

Hunting Pudding

INGREDIENTS

8 eggs

500g/1lb plain flour

500g/1lb currants

115g/4oz mixed peel

75ml/1/8pint brandy or rum

600ml/1pint cream

500g/1lb beef suet

250g/8oz raisins

115g/4oz cane sugar

A grating of nutmeg

METHOD

Beat the eggs and mix them with the cream and flour. Beat this mixture well and add finely-chopped suet, currants, peel, raisins (stoned and chopped), nutmeg and sugar. Mix in the brandy or rum. Place it into a cloth (first wetting cloth in boiling water and then sprinkling it with flour) and boil it for four hours. Take it out of cloth and cover it with sugar. Serves 10 – 12 people.

Potato Pudding

Ingredients

1kg/2lbs potatoes

250g/8oz fresh butter

8 egg yolks

3 whites of an egg stiffly whipped

250g/8oz castor sugar

300ml/½ pint of white wine or about half this amount of cooking sherry

½ grated nutmeg

300ml/½ of cream

500g/1lb puff pastry

Method

Boil the potatoes until they are soft and mash them or put them through a sieve. Add melted butter and the beaten yolks of egg. Then add the egg whites, sugar and wine, stirring well. Grate in nutmeg, then stir in the cream. Line the bottom and sides of a deep dish with the puff pastry, pour in the mixture and bake until a golden brown in a medium hot oven. Takes about 1½ hours. Serves 10 – 12 people.

Potato Pudding - CC

Plum Heavies

INGREDIENTS

250g8oz self-raising flour

¼ tsp salt, 85g/3oz lard

85g/3oz butter

100g/3½oz currants

55g/2oz soft brown sugar

About 100ml/3½oz milk

Beaten egg for glazing

METHOD

First, sift together the flour and salt. Cut the fat into small pieces or grate it coarsely. Rub about 55g/2oz of the fat into the flour. Add the currants and sugar and, using a palette knife, combine them with milk. Don't pour all the milk in at once – just use enough to combine. Turn the dough out onto a lightly floured surface and knead it lightly and be sure not to overwork it. Shape the pastry into a rough slab and roll it out to form a rectangle about 30 x12cm/12 x 6ins. Flake about 40g/1½oz of the remaining fat over the bottom two-thirds of the dough. Fold the un-fatty top third down onto the fatty middle third, then fold the fatty bottom third up. Rotate it 90 degrees then roll out again to about the same size and repeat the process with another 40g/1½oz of fat. Give it one final fold in the same way with the last of fat. Then, wrap the dough in plastic and let it rest in the fridge for about 45 minutes or a little longer. Next, preheat the oven to 200c/180C fan/gas mark 6. Roll out the dough about 6mm thick. Cut out 6.5cm/2½rounds. Then place on greased or lined baking sheets and brush with beaten egg or milk.

Collect up the scraps and roll them out again. Cut more rounds, until you've used all the dough. Bake for about 15 minutes or until it's a good golden-brown colour. Finally, cool on a wire rack.

Plum Heavies - CC Daniel Etherington

Local Customs

A shepherd in a traditional frock, c.1912
West Sussex Past picture archive

ALL ABUZZ ABOUT BEES

Bees are the focus of much Sussex folklore. 'Telling the bees' is an old custom which involves informing the family's bees of any births, marriages or deaths.

A member of the family must approach the hives and knock three times with the back door key, chanting *'The master is dead'* or *'The mistress has a baby son'*, or whatever is appropriate. In some areas the custom is to tie a black crêpe bow on each hive in the case of a death in the family. If these courtesies are not followed, the tradition goes, the bees will fly off or die.

An old man of CROWLINK, near EAST DEAN, was asked if he had heard of the custom. *'Well, I 'adent afore my old dad died,'* he replied. *'He kept bees. And I was a-going down the village street when a man said, "Have you told his bees?" "No," I says, "I ain't. I've got enough to do without a-telling of his bees." The man replied, "If you had a told them I would have bought 'em, but they won't be no good now." And they weren't – they all died.'*

Sussex folk also use the swarming of bees to foretell the future. If a swarm settles on a living bough of a tree, the family will continue in health and good fortune. If, however, the swarm settles on a piece of dead wood, there will be a death in the family. The following rhyme also applies:

A swarm of bees in May is worth a load of hay.

A swarm of bees in June is worth a silver spoon.
A swarm of bees in July is not worth a butterfly.

Sussex bees were sometimes even included in the Twelfth Night tradition of *wassailing*, more usually associated with apple trees. The hives were the focus of singing, horn-blowing and ale-drinking in honour of the bees, to wake them up and encourage honey production in the coming year.

GOODING

GOODING, or GOODENING, was a Sussex tradition whereby the elderly women of a parish would travel from house to house on ST THOMAS' DAY, 21st December, asking for gifts or 'goods' to help them through the festive season to come. Everyone would give according to their trade or their means – the miller would give a little bit of flour, the butcher a scrap of beef and so on, while from those not in trade a donation of money was expected. Widows would get a double ration.

When the Gooders had done the rounds of the local houses they would move to the church, where legacies or collections were doled out. In some places the women had to bring a small offering in exchange for their goods – an evergreen twig or a small branch from a tree.

THE WITCH OF DITCHLING

The village of DITCHLING, just north of BRIGHTON, is famous for its witch, who features in various stories. She apparently lived in a cottage called JACK O'SPADES on DITCHLING COMMON, and in one story she is credited with the ability to change into a hare. One night she did this, but she was attacked by a gang of man with dogs and bitten on the leg before she managed to escape by jumping through the window of her cottage.

The next morning she was seen nursing her leg, or (in another version of the tale) going to one of the village grandmothers to have it bandaged.

LISTEN FOR THE CUCKOO

In Sussex, *gowks*, or cuckoos, are surrounded with more folklore than any other bird. Locals are advised to turn a penny over in their pocket when they hear the first gowk in spring, to ensure they are never short of a penny in the year to come. Alternatively, they may prefer to take that penny out of their pocket and proceed directly to the nearest inn, where they must drink the bird's health.

RINGING THE BULL

Drunk or not, *ringing the bull* was a traditional pub game played in Sussex inns around LEWES and UCKFIELD. Players sat with their back to the wall

Charcoal burners near Hastings, c.1890
George Woods, East Sussex Library Archive

below a huge mounted bull's head with a hook embedded in its nose. A string was hung from the ceiling a few feet in front of the bull, with a ring on the end of it. The object of the game was to swing and throw the ring so that it landed on the hook in the bull's nose. An alternative version had the men standing some six or eight feet away and swinging the ring on its cord; some local men were so skilful that they could do this with their backs turned, and many a stranger would have been caught and made to stand a round of drinks!

Locals outside the Jolly Fisherman pub
at Sidlesham, near Chichester, c.1905
West Sussex Past picture archive

From Ash Wednesday until Good Friday, men all across Sussex would cast aside all their other pub games and bring out their prize marbles, competing in teams across the county until Good Friday *(or Marbles Day)*, when the local finals would be played, often in the porch of the church (or the churchyard if the weather was fine). The games finished on the dot of twelve noon, when the midday service would commence in the church; if any games continued after that time, it was quite legitimate for opposing players to jump on the marbles with cries of *'Goblins!'*, *'Scrabbles!'* or *'Smugs!'*, claiming them as their own.

Loading the hay at Amberley, near Worthing, c.1890
West Sussex Past picture archive

Ghost Stories
TALES OF THE SUPERNATURAL TO CHILL THE BLOOD

PRESTON MANOR

The accolade of most haunted house in Brighton and Hove is often given to Preston Manor.

With parts of the interior dating back to the 1200s, this largely 18th-century mansion was formerly to be found in the village of Preston, which has since been swallowed up by the modern conurbation. The house is now a museum evoking the life of the upper classes during the Edwardian period. Preston Manor's traditional ghost is that of a 'WHITE LADY'. A séance held in 1896 suggested that the ghost was that of a nun, who had been excommunicated and then executed for some past misdemeanour.

When a woman's skeleton was later unearthed in the garden it was reburied in the nearby churchyard. Whether the bones belonged to the nun are unclear, for when the White Lady subsequently appeared to an army officer, telling him she had been wrongly excommunicated, she had no knowledge of having been buried in consecrated ground. Masses for her soul were arranged nonetheless but, since she continues to haunt Preston Manor, we must assume they did not satisfy her.

Preston Manor is considered by many to be Brighton and Hove's most haunted house. © Marq English

The house has become popular with ghost-hunting groups in recent years and a further range of spooky goings-on have been reported, especially eerie sounds such as moaning, groaning, a child's sobbing and the voices of adults raised in anger. Further apparitions include a 'GREY LADY', a disembodied hand floating in a darkened bedroom, and a possible sighting of a spectral dog.

BRIGHTON ROYAL PAVILION

By far the most famous haunted house in Brighton and Hove, however, is surely the ROYAL PAVILION. The Pavilion was built on the orders of the PRINCE REGENT, later GEORGE IV, as a summer retreat and 'pleasure palace'. Orientalism was at its height at the

The opulent Royal Pavilion, haunted by the man who ordered it to be built, King George IV, among other ghosts - iStock

time and the building is a fantastic concoction of Indian-style domes and minarets, with a riot of Chinese-inspired decoration inside it. SAMUEL JOHNSON unkindly said of the Pavilion that *'it looked for all the world as if the Dome of St Paul's [Cathedral] had come down to Brighton and pupped'*. Today its extravagant architecture and lavish interior attract thousands of visitors every year.

ghost was later identified as that of MARTHA GUNN, an enthusiastic *'dipper'* who helped popularise sea-bathing at Brighton. A little private staircase leading from the King's Apartment is haunted by a spectral servant.

Outside, in the gardens, a much more gruesome ghost has been encountered. This is the spectre of a hideously decaying body, with ghostly maggots writhing in its empty eye-sockets. This is supposed to represent JOHN ROBINSON, a mercenary who had his eyes put out for supporting a failed rebellion in the Middle East. He was found begging in the street by an Englishman, who brought him back to Brighton. But Robinson died almost as soon as his feet touched his home soil, in the place now occupied by the Pavilion's grounds.

The pudgy but elegant figure of GEORGE IV has been known to promenade in the art gallery. The apparition of a large lady in a floppy hat has been seen walking round the banqueting table as if trying to find her place. The

EASTBOURNE PIER

Eastbourne's pier, in common with those at Brighton, is believed to be haunted. Author JANET CAMERON interviewed a member of the pier staff who claimed to have witnessed a range of paranormal activity here, including the sighting of an apparition, apparently of a man in a black cape and wearing a 'trilby-type hat'. Further witnesses reported strange goings-on in the Atlantis nightclub. The ghosts of a woman in black, a soldier in the uniform of the SECOND WORLD WAR and a morose child have been seen. The venue has also experienced weird lights and sounds and the inexplicable behaviour of electrical equipment.

A considerable amount of paranormal activity has been reported from Eastbourne's 19th-century pier. iStock

Worthing, where ghost-hunter Andrew Green was offered a cup of tea by a ghost - iStock

THE HAUNTED B&B

When paranormal investigator ANDREW GREEN decided to stay the night in Worthing, he found he'd accidentally chosen a haunted B&B. The incident, which he relates in his book *Our Haunted Kingdom*, took place in 1951. He writes: *'I was woken by a young lad bringing in a cup of tea. I thanked him, but finding the liquid cold and horribly sweet looked up at him to make some comment to find that he had gone. He had appeared to be very ill with a small thin grey haggard little face and huge brown eyes like saucers accentuated by dark circles. What heightened his general appearance of misery and neglect was the bedraggled older style brown suit that hung rag-like from his shoulders.'*

When he mentioned his experience to the guest house's owners, they were as puzzled as he was, since there were no children in the house and it wasn't their policy to bring cups of tea to their boarders in the morning. They did suggest that the cold tea might have been left there from the previous night and presumably thought Mr Green was a rather confused gentleman who had had a dream. However, when Green spoke privately to the regular boarders he learned that a few of them had shared his experience on previous occasions. The incident remained a mystery.

Bognor Ghouls

ARRON WEEDALL recounts a number of ghost stories from BOGNOR REGIS in his book *Haunted Chichester and Beyond*, including accounts of another haunted pier, the fourth reported in Sussex. Mr Weedall's research reveals that the ghost of *'an old-looking man with dark hair'* has been seen in a nightclub on the pier. The nearby PICTUREDROME CINEMA, which opened in 1919 when the movies were silent, black-and-white and strictly 2D, has a ghostly cinephile, who strolls about the auditorium and has been known to sit in one of the seats, usually when

there is nothing on the screen. Of course, if he chose to sit in the cinema while a movie was showing, how would anyone know, in the dark, that there wasn't a ghost sitting beside them?

Ghost Fights in Rye

The MERMAID INN is a magnificent, timber-framed and ivy-clad hostelry dating back to the early 15th century, although another structure may have been on the same site from the 1100s. It is probably RYE'S most haunted building. Its most famous ghost is that of two sword-fighters in doublet and hose who manifest in Room 16. After a fierce fight, one of the men is run through and the other drags the corpse to the corner of the room. After that, the show is over and the ghosts vanish.

Further ghosts include a chubby gent who sits on the ends of people's beds and a young woman who was murdered in the 18th century by a notorious gang of smugglers. In Room 1 guests have seen a female form sitting in a chair by the fireplace. Garments left on this chair were sometimes found to have become unaccountably wet overnight. Outside, in Mermaid Street, apparitions of women in costumes of the medieval period have been seen.

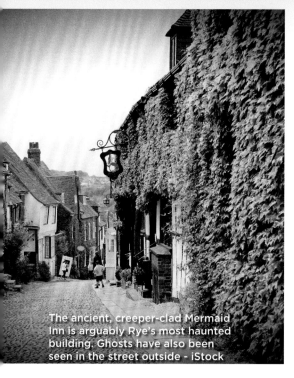

The ancient, creeper-clad Mermaid Inn is arguably Rye's most haunted building. Ghosts have also been seen in the street outside - iStock

THE STRANGE HISTORY OF COWDRAY HOUSE

That the splendid COWDRAY HOUSE, near MIDHURST, should now be found in ruins might be considered proof of the terrible curse that fell upon it in the 16th century. During the Dissolution of the Monasteries, the owner of Cowdray, SIR ANTHONY BROWNE, evicted all the monks then in residence at BATTLE ABBEY. Browne was promptly cursed by one of the disgruntled monks. As he was being booted off the premises he cried out: *'By fire and by water thy line shall come to an end and it shall perish out of the land!'*

The curse took some time to come into effect – more than two hundred years, in fact. In 1793 disaster – indeed several disasters – struck. Cowdray was being redecorated in time for the wedding of Sir Anthony's descendant, the VISCOUNT MONTAGUE, but a spark from a brazier started a blaze that left the grand house in ruins. While this calamity was occurring, the bridegroom-to-be was enjoying his last few weeks as a bachelor with a friend in Germany. The young viscount was a bit of a daredevil and he and his friend unwisely attempted to shoot some rapids on the RIVER RHINE, with the result that both of them drowned. The curse had come upon Cowdray through the mediums of fire and water, as predicted. The next heir was a childless Catholic priest. His two nephews, who inherited Cowdray on his death, were also drowned, at Bognor. This line of the Browne family had now been extinguished and Cowdray has remained a ruin.

When DAVID SCANLAN visited the remains of Cowdray House while researching his book *Paranormal Sussex*, he learned of at least two ghosts. One is said to be the wife of the fifth Viscount Montague, who shot dead a priest for having the temerity to starting Mass without him. He spent the remainder of his life in hiding, ironically enough in a priest hole. The ghost of his long-suffering wife is seen walking towards Cowdray from Midhurst. Between the ruined mansion and the new Cowdray House (the present home of LORD AND LADY COWDRAY) there is a path which has become known as Lady's Walk after the ghost which patrols it. She is believed to be the widow of the cursed Sir Anthony Browne. Browne himself may have haunted his former bedroom, but the haunting came to an end with the fire.

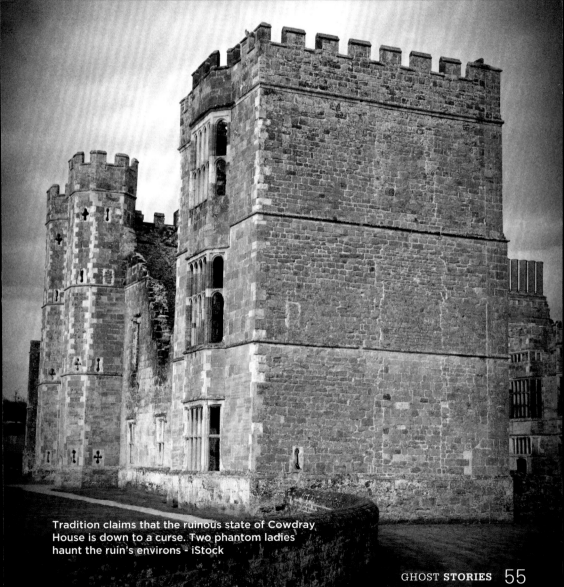

Tradition claims that the ruinous state of Cowdray House is down to a curse. Two phantom ladies haunt the ruin's environs - iStock

Sussex Legends

FARMING AND THE LAND

Sussex is a heavily forested county, with many vestiges of ancient woodland still surviving from the primeval forest of the Weald. In combination with the rural heritage of the county, it's not surprising that there is a great deal of tree and nature lore in the minds and language of the people.

Elder trees have long been thought to be the home of fairies, and it was considered polite to ask the resident's permission if a tree needed chopping down or trimming. Even relatively recently a woman who lived by the PEVENSEY MARSHES was warned by her husband as she chopped down an elder tree: 'Have you asked old Hobbledick if you can do that? The old people round here say that if you don't, you'll have bad luck!'

Elder wood is also known to be particularly good for fencing and hedging purposes – it is said that an elder stake in the ground will last as long as an iron bar. An old Sussex saying goes:

> An eldern stake and blackthorn ether,
> Will make a hedge that lasts forever.

AS CLEAR AS MUD

Sussex mud is legendary. It is well known to be an especially viscous and sticky sort of mud, particularly across the Weald, and is generally considered to be far superior to anything that other counties can produce.

There are many Sussex stories involving mud. Legend has it that

A muddy Sussex road near Hastings, c.1890
George Woods, East Sussex Library Archive

the women and beasts of Sussex have particularly long legs, developed because of the effort of striding through the glutinous stuff: *'Why is it that the oxen, the swine, the women and all other animals, are so long-legged in Sussex? May it be from the difficulty of pulling the feet out of so much mud by the strength of the ankle that the muscles get stretched, as it were, and the bones lengthened?'*

One of the best-known tales, often repeated and connected with various parts of the county, concerns a man who was walking along a muddy lane and came across a hat lying on the ground. He stooped to lift it up, and was surprised to find a head beneath it. Being a polite sort of fellow he enquired after the health of the head's owner, commenting that he must be finding his present situation a little uncomfortable.

'Nay,' came the reply, *'not nearly so uncomfortable as the man whose shoulders I'm standing on, nor yet the horse that he is riding.'*

Sussex folk have a wide and descriptive vocabulary for classifying the mud of their county. Mud may be CLODGY (muddy and wet), GAWM (sticky and foul-smelling) or SLABBY (sticky, slippery and greasy). GUBBER is a particularly unpleasant type of black mud made of rotting organic matter, while sleech is river sediment sometimes used as manure. SLOB is thick mud, but slab is the thickest sort; in contrast, SLURRY is diluted mud, saturated with water. An IKE is a mess or area of mud, while a SLOUGH is a muddy hole and a SWANK is a bog. If the INUIT PEOPLES have a rich vocabulary for describing snow and ice, the Sussex folk may certainly be considered as running them a close second in terms of mud.

COUNTING SHEEP

Sheep are an integral part of the upland rural scene; generations of shepherds have trodden the grass of THE DOWNS to tend their flocks. Some West Sussex shepherds counted their sheep in pairs as they ran them into the fold, rather than singly as in other regions. As the pairs of sheep ran past, the shepherd would count them in as follows:

One-erum, two-erum, cock-erum,
shu-erum, sith-erum,
Sath-erum, wineberry, wagtail,
tarrydiddle, den

Since they were counted in pairs, arriving at den meant the shepherd had counted twenty sheep. A notch would be made on the shepherd's tally stick, and the counting would begin again.

Other areas of the county had their own counting rhymes – this one goes up to twenty, with a clear reminder to tally (or cut a notch on the stick) when twenty is reached:

> Wintherum, wontherum, twintherum,
> twontherum, wagtail,
> Whitebelly, coram, dar, diddle, den,
> Etherum, atherum, shootherum,
> cootherum, windbar,
> Bobtail, inadik, dyadic, bumpit,
> ecack-tally.

SHEPHERDS' TALES

Sussex shepherds set a great deal of store by SHEPHERD'S CROWNS, or fossilised sea urchins, as protection against thunderstorms. It was a foolish shepherd who didn't carry one of these small stones in his pocket, and when a storm rolled in

A shepherd with his dog and flock on the South Downs above Steyning, near Worthing, c.1910 West Sussex Past picture archive

over the Downs shepherds out on the hills would hold the urchin tightly for protection. If kept indoors, they were also believed to protect houses from catching fire or being struck by lightning.

Sussex shepherds were highly particular about female visitors to their lambing folds. One said, *'Boss's wife be too fond o' poken' 'bout here. If I got a ewe as wants a doctor, I fastens t'wattle tight. I wunt have women lookin' on while I be doctor, fur 't'int decent!'*

OLD DICK was a well-known local character around Horsham, a simpleton whose eccentric and amusing escapades and sayings were passed around with a great deal of glee. Once a farmer paid Dick to work on his farm for a few days, helping with the sheep. After a while the farmer came to check on what Dick was up to.

'Have you counted those sheep yet, Dick?' he asked.

'Yep,' came the reply. *'I counted 'em all but one, but 'ee run about so much, I couldn't count of 'ee.*

Two farm labourers takin' a bit o' coger, near Hastings, c.1890 George Woods, East Sussex Library Archive

Murder MYSTERIES

Real Sussex Murders

MURDER ON THE BRIGHTON TRAIN

It was late in the afternoon of 27th June 1881 when 22-year-old Percy Lefroy Mapleton staggered out of the train at Preston Park station.

He was ruffled and splattered with blood and was claiming that he had been attacked by two men. Over the next few hours it emerged that in fact Mapleton himself had committed a murder on the Brighton train. But by the time the truth was known Mapleton had disappeared.

Once a week 64-year-old ISAAC FREDERICK GOLD, a former stockbroker living in CLERMONT TERRACE in BRIGHTON, would travel to London to attend to his business. On that June afternoon in 1881 he was travelling on the 2.10pm train from LONDON, expecting to arrive back at PRESTON PARK by 3.30pm.

Soon to travel on the same train was MAPLETON, who was a failed author, journalist and actor from CARSHALTON in SURREY. By the time of the murder he was heavily in debt and on the verge of bankruptcy. Now, armed with a revolver, knife and what little money he had left, Mapleton travelled to LONDON BRIDGE STATION and purchased a first-class single ticket to BRIGHTON.

Mapleton left the train briefly at EAST CROYDON and walked along the

MURDER **STORIES** 61

platform past the first-class section of the train until he spotted Mr Gold, who was sitting alone in a carriage. Mapleton sat opposite with every intention of committing a robbery as soon as he had the opportunity. To avoid witnesses and the possibility of anyone hearing a scuffle or gunshots, he decided to act once the train entered one of the tunnels on the route. In committing the robbery it seems that Mapleton fired three or four shots, but this was still insufficient to kill Mr Gold, who put up a ferocious fight for his life. Finally, in Balcombe Tunnel, which is two-thirds of the way to Brighton, Mapleton managed to open the carriage door and force the dead or dying Mr Gold out of the compartment and on to the track.

It turned out that Percy had not chosen the best victim. As well as the desperate struggle he had put up, it now seemed that Mr Gold had very little money on him. What he had Percy took, along with Mr Gold's watch. Mapleton now had to get rid of as much evidence as possible. Percy threw his revolver, bloodstained collar and other incriminating evidence out of the window and concocted the story of having himself been the victim of an attack.

Despite the suspicious lack of any assailants and the shocking bloodstained appearance of the train carriage, at first everyone was sympathetic to Percy's plight. After providing statements and completing other formalities it was arranged for him to be accompanied back to London. Certainly there was concern for his injuries, but there was already some suspicion that everything was not quite as he had described it.

Soon two railway workers discovered Mr Gold's body in Balcombe Tunnel. The railwaymen quickly left the tunnel to report their find, but the news of the discovery did not reach Mapleton's entourage, now bound for London or, for that matter, Mr Gold's wife, who waited dutifully for the return of her husband at Preston Park station.

After giving his companions the slip, Percy attempted to cover his tracks further. He threw the stolen watch off Blackfriars Bridge and attempted to lie low. However, within 24 hours of Percy's escape, *'Wanted for Murder'* police notices describing him began appearing all over London. Soon these were superseded by further posters, now offering a £200 reward for his arrest. Then, with Mapleton still proving elusive, the DAILY TELEGRAPH published an artist's impression of the fugitive. This was a new technique and while it created plenty of public interest it also resulted in alleged sightings of Mapleton all over the country.

It was now nearly a fortnight since the attack and throughout this time Percy had been hiding in STEPNEY under an assumed name. Now, desperately short of money, he broke cover and sent a telegram to his old employer asking for his wages to be sent to his lodgings at 32 SMITH STREET. The resulting knock on the door did not bring Mapleton the expected money; instead it was two police inspectors and he was placed under arrest.

Percy Lefroy Mapleton before the magistrates in Cuckfield - CC

On 4th November 1881 Mapleton stood trial before LORD CHIEF JUSTICE COLERIDGE at the MAIDSTONE ASSIZES. He pleaded not guilty but it took the jury just ten minutes to decide that he was. While awaiting execution Mapleton made a series of statements providing a bewildering variety of confessions to Mr Gold's murder, each inventing different motives and methods. Eventually, having tired of his own case, he started confessing to other unsolved crimes, none of which could have contained any truth. Mapleton was hanged for the murder on the Brighton train in LEWES on 29th November 1881.

THE POISONED CHOCOLATES CASE

It was in the early 1870s that Christiana Edmunds conducted her poisoning campaign.

She attempted to poison her lover's wife and several other people in Brighton before adopting a more random approach. She obtained chocolate creams and, after lacing them with strychnine, would return them to the shop from where they had been bought. The shopkeeper, not knowing them to be poisoned, would then sell them a second time. It was by this means that Christiana was to murder SIDNEY BARKER.

Christiana Edmunds was born in Margate in 1828. She lived for some years in CANTERBURY. But it was after moving to GLOUCESTER PLACE in Brighton, with her widowed mother, that she met and became infatuated by DR CHARLES BEARD, who lived at 64 GRAND PARADE with his wife EMILY and their children.

When Charles attempted to end their relationship, Christiana had visited the Beards' house with a gift of chocolates for Emily. The following day Mrs Beard became violently ill, but fortunately recovered. Dr Beard had his suspicions that she had been poisoned but he was desperate to keep his relationship with Christiana secret and so did not report the incident.

Edmunds carried on with her activities unabated. Using the alias of MISS

WOOD from KINGSTON in SURREY, she was obtaining the strychnine from a chemist called DR ISAAC GARRETT, who was based in the QUEEN'S ROAD. This was done on the pretence that she needed it to poison cats that had been making a mess in her garden. This was not the greatest cover story as Dr Garrett didn't like the sound of his strychnine being used in that way and told her that she would have to get her poison elsewhere. Next time Christiana visited Garrett she changed her story and said that she was in fact going to poison a dog. Now banned from the chemist on the grounds of cruelty, Christiana managed to get her supply of strychnine through a dressmaker friend called CAROLINE STONE who acted on her behalf.

Soon she was using another emissary, a boy named ADAM MAY, to purchase the chocolates on her behalf since she was starting to draw too much attention to herself with her constant purchases. May simply believed that he was running an innocent errand for Christiana.

While several people in Brighton had become ill, no one had connected the illnesses with the chocolates. That was until June 1871 when the BARKER FAMILY came on a day trip to Brighton. UNCLE CHARLES visited MAYNARDS, the confectioners, thinking that some sweets would be a nice present for four-year-old SIDNEY. Several members of the family ate a chocolate and found the distinctive metallic flavour not to their taste and spat them out. Unfortunately Sidney did not do the same.

A verdict of 'accidental death' was recorded by the coroner. Maynards disposed of all existing stock and was then allowed to resume trading. Also conducting business as usual was Christiana.

Dr Beard, still estranged from Christiana, was watching from afar and finally could not keep quiet any longer. Following his statement, the police came to interview Christiana. They were to find her reclining on a couch at her mother's house, supposedly too feeble to stand after eating a poisoned apricot from a basket of fruit sent to her by a deranged poisoner. The police were not fooled and she was soon charged with the attempted murder of Emily Beard.

At Christiana's trial at the OLD BAILEY in January 1872, her mother testified that both sides of their family had a history of mental illness. Dr Beard was to claim that he and Edmunds never had a proper relationship, but that instead it was merely a series of flirtatious letters sent by her to him. The defence, however, was able to indicate that the two had in fact become involved in an affair, arguing that it was this that had sent Edmunds over the edge into madness.

It took the jury only an hour to deliver their verdict. Then there was a further hour needed to disprove Christiana's dramatic assertion that she was pregnant. At last the judge sentenced Christiana to death, but this was then commuted to life imprisonment due to her mental state.

After the trial things returned to normal in Brighton. Dr Beard and his family remained in Brighton and by the 1890s they were living in GERMAN PLACE, which is now MADEIRA PLACE, just off the seafront. Meanwhile Christiana was to spend the rest of her days in BROADMOOR, where she was to die in 1907.

Famous **Names**

THE BODY SHOP

One of the high street's best-loved stores began its fascinating history in BRIGHTON. Now based in LITTLEHAMPTON, **The Body Shop** is a British cosmetics, skincare and perfume company. Founded in 1976 by DAME ANITA RODDICK, it currently has a range of 1,000 products selling in 3,000 franchised stores in no fewer than 66 countries! What made The Body Shop different from the outset was its stance on providing ethically sourced and produced cosmetics. The company was also a leader in social activism, working with GREENPEACE to help save whales. The Body Shop has campaigned to end animal testing in cosmetics since 1989 and all its products are now non-animal tested and certified cruelty-free. There is little doubt that this enduringly uncompromising approach has helped to shape public attitudes towards shopping more ethically.

TELEVISION

Thanks to JOHN LOGIE BAIRD, the very first working television set came to life in a workshop in LINTON CRESCENT, HASTINGS and then in the QUEEN'S ARCADE in HASTINGS. These important achievements followed many years of effort by other inventors as well as Baird. Baird had actually moved to Hastings due to ill health, but still ended up achieving that major milestone in TV history. It is said that he found inspiration during an afternoon stroll across the cliff tops at FAIRLIGHT GLEN. The world's first working TV set, known as the televisor, was made of items including an old hatbox, some darning needles and sealing wax and glue!

John Logie Baird - CC

In February 1924, Baird demonstrated to the RADIO TIMES that it was possible to create a semi-mechanical analogue television system by transmitting moving silhouette images. After receiving a 1,000-volt electric shock, but surviving with only a burnt hand, Baird was asked to vacate the premises by his landlord and moved to London where he completed his work on the television. However, he did return to the south coast in 1944, setting up home in BEXHILL, where he lived up until his death two years later.

ONLINE SHOPPING

Back in 1979, being able to order goods via a computer sounded like something out of a science fiction movie. But it was while walking with his wife in COLGATE that Sussex-based MICHAEL ALDRICH hit upon the idea. This came after having a TV delivered to his office and a subsequent conversation about doing the shopping. Inspired, Aldrich connected a modified domestic television via a telephone line to a computer. He then marketed his systems from 1980 onwards and they were installed in the UK, Ireland and Spain. Aldrich's work led to a number of important world firsts. He was very much ahead of his time. Business-to-consumer

iStock

online shopping as we know it now was not viable until the widespread use of computers and of course the internet in the 1990s. Sadly, while Aldrich gained great fame for his achievements in the 80s, he was forgotten two decades later, with many of his ideas being copied.

Aldrich was an innovator in other ways too. He helped to shape large-scale data capture, mixed media scanning, minicomputer networking, voice response and handprint processing. In fact, he was the first person to patent a static signature recognition system. Thankfully, he has gained more public recognition in recent years. In June 2011, an ICM Poll in the UK voted Aldrich's date of birth, 22 August 1941, as the seventh most important date in the history of the internet. So, next time you're surfing the online shops, spare a thought for that first moment of inspiration which came to Michael Aldrich as he went walking in Colgate.

Sussex *Sport*

CRICKET

Sussex is the birthplace of cricket. It is thought that the sport was first invented by children who lived on the Weald as far back as Anglo-Saxon or Norman times!

Cricket was a much-loved game played in many local villages. The game really took off in the county in the 17th century. At BOXMOOR in 1622, six locals were prosecuted for playing cricket in the churchyard on Sunday! It is thought that the first county teams were created after the Restoration in 1660. The very first cricket match was recorded in the *Foreign Post* in 1697, involving an eleven-a-side game in Sussex. The first recorded inter-county match took place in August 1735 at Sevenoaks in Kent. This involved a game between SIR WILLIAM GAGE OF FIRLE and ten other Sussex men, and the EARL OF MIDDLESEX, the LORD JOHN SACKVILLE and nine other men from Kent. The game grew yet more popular in Sussex. In 1791, the PRINCE OF WALES, as he was then (before he became GEORGE IV) presented a cricket ground to Brighton. In 1836, **Sussex Cricket Club** was formed. Today it is proud to be England's oldest county cricket club.

Stoolball

Sussex is the home of a sport called **Stoolball**. This is an ancient game that dates back as far as 1450. Rather than being a traditionally competitive sport, it is thought to have taken place as part of early courtship rituals during Easter celebrations. It was played by milkmaids who used their milking stools as a kind of wicket. SAMUEL JOHNSON mentions the game in his dictionary. Some believe it to be related to cricket, baseball and rounders and it is sometimes known by the rather poetic name of *'cricket in the air'!* It requires eleven players on each side who play in very similar positions to those of cricket.

Down in a vale on a summer's day
All the lads and lasses met to be merry,
A match for kisses at stool-ball to play,
And for cakes, and ale, and cider
and perry.

SONG FROM 1694

The Little Pretty Pocket Book by Isaiah Thomas (1767) depicts men playing stoolball - CC

Later on, the game became more formal with the stools being replaced by wickets mounted on posts or stakes. It went through quite a revival during WORLD WAR I when it was played by injured soldiers recovering from the war. However, it became less popular until much more recently. These days, stoolball is played by local leagues in KENT, SURREY and the MIDLANDS, as well as in SUSSEX. It was recognised as a sport by the SPORTS COUNCIL in early 2008. You can find some fascinating footage of a 1951 game played in Sussex by visiting **https://www.britishpathe.com/video/stoolball**.

LEWES WORLD PEA THROWING CHAMPIONSHIP

Think you're good at lobbing vegetables? Then you might want to participate in the annual **Pea Throwing Championships** which take place at the LEWES ARMS every October. The game is played by throwing three frozen peas down CASTLE DITCH LANE next to the pub. To win, you have to be the person whose pea travels the furthest! The best distance achieved so far is an impressive 44 metres!

LONG-ROPE SKIPPING

Sussex was known for its long-established tradition of skipping with long ropes on Good Friday. While the activity once took place in a number of locations such as BRIGHTON and LEWES, the only surviving event takes place by the ROSE COTTAGE INN at ALCISTON. It is thought to have originally formed part of a ritual to help encourage the crops to grow well.

BRITISH AND WORLD MARBLES CHAMPIONSHIP

Peas aren't the only small round things that play an important role in the gaming prowess of Sussex. The county is also home to the **British and World Marbles Championship**. The ancient marble-playing tradition in the area goes back to special games played every Good Friday. The

iStock

competition has been played in the same format at the same place, the GREYHOUND PUBLIC HOUSE in TINSLEY GREEN in WEST SUSSEX, since 1932. Teams of six battle it out in a marbles knock-out tournament to win the title and a silver trophy. Curiously enough, love is the cause of this internationally popular event. The story goes that in 1588 a game of marbles was used to decide which of two suitors would win the hand of a milkmaid called JOAN. Instead of simply asking Joan which suitor she would prefer, the gentlemen fought it out in a host of games, including singlestick, wrestling and quarter staff. The marbles game was the deciding factor. One wonders if the excessive competition actually made Joan question whether either suitor was really the man for her. But at least Sussex has a much-loved international tournament to show for the ancient rivalry.

iStock

Famous Locals

CAITLIN MORAN

CATHERINE ELIZABETH 'CAITLIN' MORAN is an English journalist, author and broadcaster and an important figure in modern feminism. Born in BRIGHTON in 1975, Moran and her family then moved to WOLVERHAMPTON. She had an unconventional upbringing and described her family as '*the only hippies in Wolverhampton*'. Moran changed her name to CAITLIN after seeing the name in a JILLY COOPER novel. She quickly established herself as a writer, winning the **Observer's Young Reporter of the Year** at the tender age of 15. At just 16, she began her career as a journalist for MELODY MAKER. In the early 1990s, Moran hosted the Channel 4 music show **Naked City**. She has worked as a columnist on The Times for more than twenty years.

Moran's upbringing inspired her TV drama/comedy series, the very funny *Raised by Wolves*. Her books include *How to be a Woman, How To Build a Girl, Moranthology* and *Moranifesto*. In April 2014, Moran was named as one of Britain's most influential women in the BBC WOMAN'S HOUR power list 2014. Her many accolades include **British Press Awards Columnist of the Year for 2010** and **BPA Critic of the Year 2011** and **Interviewer of the Year 2011**, the London Press Club's **Columnist of the Year** and **Culture Commentator** at the COMMENT AWARDS in 2013.

Percy Bysshe Shelley

One of the world's greatest poets was a Sussex local. Born in 1792 near Horsham, Percy Bysshe Shelley was one of the leading English Romantic poets. Shelley was a courageous, radical and short-lived character who sadly did not receive recognition for his talents in his lifetime. During his time as a student at Oxford University, Shelley started to become interested in radical writers. Later on, he was expelled from Oxford for contributing to a pamphlet that supported Atheism. Not content with this level of controversy, Shelley then eloped to Scotland with his 16-year-old love, Harriet Westbrook. While they had two children, they separated soon afterwards. He then fell for Mary, the daughter of writers William Godwin and Mary Wollstonecraft. The two travelled around Europe together

and ended up spending a summer at Lake Geneva with Lord Byron. It was here that Shelley wrote poetry and Mary developed the idea for her novel *Frankenstein*. Shortly after the suicide of Shelley's first wife, the two were married and moved to Italy. Tragically, two of their children died and Mary had a nervous breakdown. However, this proved to be the most productive period of Shelley's life. He was able to create some of his greatest works before his untimely death.

Elizabeth David

Sussex was the first home of yet another important cultural figure. While writing about food may not seem radical at first glance, Elizabeth David played an important role in reshaping the way that cookery writing was seen in the UK and the US. Born Elizabeth Gwynne in 1913 into an aristocratic family, she grew up at Wootton Manor in Sussex, a 17th-century manor house. David rebelled against the limited expectations that her family – and society – had for her. The time she spent studying art in Paris changed how she saw food for ever.

After various adventures, David returned to England and started writing articles on cookery before publishing her first book, *A Book of Mediterranean Food*. Four more Mediterranean-based books appeared in the next decade. While all her books were well received, it was her *French Provincial Cooking*, published in 1960, which really helped change attitudes and created a new appetite for French food in the UK. A shop in London and further books followed. She was appointed OBE in 1976, CBE in 1986 and elected a **Fellow of the Royal Society of Literature** in 1982. In 1977, she was appointed a **Chevalier du Merite Agricole of France**. In 1992, her obituary in the Telegraph stated: *'Her pen did not merely inspire a thousand cooks. It is largely to Mrs David that Britain owes its growing appreciation of good food.'*

ENGLISH HERITAGE
ELIZABETH DAVID
1913 ~ 1992
Cookery Writer
lived and worked here
1947 ~ 1992

CC

Leo Sayer

Leo Sayer is a Sussex-born musician and entertainer with a singing career which has spanned four decades. Now an Australian Citizen and resident, he was born in Shoreham-by-Sea in 1948. Gerard Hugh Sayer was destined to become one of the world's best-loved singers. He began singing in his local church choir and it is this experience which helped him to find his voice. As if that wasn't enough, young Gerard was also a talented artist and eventually went to the West Sussex College of Art and Design in Worthing. This is where he really started to explore his talents, spending time drawing on Worthing beach and playing the mouth organ. It was there that he met a professional harmonica player who taught him how to play.

Leo played the mouth organ on his train journey to art school every day and soon learned enough to jam with local bands. Although he moved to London, he returned home after facing some challenges in the capital. Thanks to a lot of work and to a talent contest in Brighton, his career took off. Sayer became a star in the 1970s, with hit singles and albums both in the US and UK. In fact, Sayer's first seven hit singles in the UK all reached the Top Ten. His hits include *'Moonlighting'*, *'You Make Me Feel Like Dancing'* and *'When I Need You'*.

Shoreham-by-Sea - iStock

More Bradwell Titles For You To Enjoy

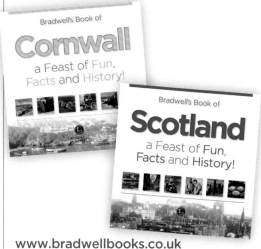

Bradwell's Book of
Cornwall
a Feast of Fun, Facts and History!

Bradwell's Book of
Scotland
a Feast of Fun, Facts and History!

www.bradwellbooks.co.uk